T0161046

Bamboophobia

Ko Ko Thett

Zephyr Press | Brookline, Mass.

Printed in Michigan by Cushing Malloy, Inc.

Zephyr Press acknowledges with gratitude the financial
support of the Massachusetts Cultural Council
and the National Endowment for the Arts.

Zephyr Press, a non-profit arts and education 501(c)(3) organization,
publishes literary titles that foster a deeper understanding of cultures
and languages. Zephyr Press books are distributed worldwide
by Consortium Book Sales and Distribution [www.cbsd.com].

Cataloguing-in publication data is available from the Library of Congress.

ISBN 978-1938890-85-7

ZEPHYR PRESS
www.zephyrpress.org

Table of Contents

for thett su san

Accent

My skin was born in the Year of the Pig. My accent much later, and it'd rather be a Capricorn. I seduce women with my accent. I subdue them with my skin.

You will still hear my skin whinge even after maggots dwell and die in my accent.

My skin is my landscape, my accent my fresh air. My skin is too thin for bad weather. My accent, so incredibly thick it whistles under water.

I am not one of those sentenced to solitary confinement for life inside their own skins. I can get under your skin once I step out of my accent.

People judge me by my skin. My skin's purpose in life is to prove them wrong. Once I open my mouth my accent proves them right. I keep my mouth shut, my skin open.

Which is truer, my skin or my accent? When it comes to swinishness they are on the same page.

In places where I am considered white, my yellow accent always holds me back. Since whatever comes from my mouth is an unpasteurized lie, I will always have a yellow accent.

As for my skin—

it will be blues when it fancies the blues;

it will be jazz when it fancies jazz.

Let us suppose you love me

§   Leaves and twigs on the ground

Do I have to know the name of that tall tree to freefall from her
canopy? In my language there are 1,500 synonyms for penis,
and only 528 different ways to describe vagina.
Does that say anything about my phobia?

§   Let me break it down again

Shall I collapse into a relapse? I am a bambino taking his first
steps. White lotus blooms from the earth just to embrace each
of my footfalls.

Off-balance, I keep smiling to myself. This moment, I am gold.
Next moment, I am silver. Before bedtime each day, I take a pill
that only dissolves in my liver.

§   Cane, in fact, is a little brother of bamboo

In the Liberated Area, I lived on bamboo shoots in a bamboo
hut. I carried a bamboo rifle. The Thais say the weapons of
choice of the royal Burmese infantry that ransacked Siam in
the 18th century were solid bamboo clubs and bamboo spears.
I have seen throats cut with a bamboo strip on the China
border.

At school I was caned by my language teachers. At home I was caned by my father. In the Liberated Area, they stripped me naked, they crammed me in a bamboo coop and, with a tiny wet cane, struck the most sensual parts of my body day in and day out until I could name all 1,500 synonyms for penis. Rebooting never cleanses my system of bamboophobia. A famine is imminent whenever bamboos flower.

§   They say fuck because all the other four-letter words were taken

Life's trappings are deeper than the Pacific Ocean's Mariana trench. A German lover who once proposed to me said the only reason she wanted to get married was for a new name. Her family name translates as Taxcollector. Recently she has become Frau Wagner, Mrs. Wagondriver.

§   I recommend you walk around in Rangoon's diagonal rain

That'll correct your neck pain. If you climb, you can climb to the canopy. If you dive, you'd better dive to the sand and avoid hitting rock bottom. If you are into diving—as opposed to climbing—which most of us do since our ancestors left the ocean, Hla Than has warned, "Never take the earth for granted. I have come to understand art after having sex with a transsexual who is more woman than woman."

Pollen fever

*

Contrary to what they believed, I was never allergic to skins.
Or sunrays. I wasn't a cadre.

**

Arrested by three. Tortured by five. Fornication. For negligence.
For negation. Wasn't that a question about syzygy? Or posture?
He'd even pawned his pearls to pose with my wax figure.
I sneezed profusely in their hands.

***

First they spoke a language that embraced you like a failed state.
Then they switched.

Like a passage from winter to summer, the transition was
ungovernable, and violent.

****

Damn you all! Indecent infixes, triple consonants and doted vowels!
Like Mi Aye, I've had it twice.
Once for being too yellow.
Once for being too white.

*****

Even after they'd renamed pollen fever hay fever, I insisted watchful
trees mustn't bloom. Rain may settle dust, but leave us with wet pyres.
For padauk, however, a drizzle is never enough.

We go faster uphill

Winter is upon me, light as lint, unforgetful as squirrels.
The Roselles wear red today. No wonder they're related to
the Hibiscuses! Potatoes can't wait to sprout in my kitchen.

The Orient has taught me a thing or two. Life begins in a womb
for rent. Purchase for purchase. At market frontiers. If you
want to have an affair you must be as close-lipped as a fart in
a whirlpool. People in The Dark Ages didn't call their days
The Dark Ages. Horses do not find discomfort in a horsehide
saddle.

The Occident has taught me a thing or two. Once, his mistake.
Twice, yours. Thrice, you are the fart in the whirlpool.

Blood begets blood. Margot begets Margot. Cross when the
light is green. Double-cross when the Roselles are red.

What really happened to me at Laizastrasse

- Mykonos, the Greek restaurant on the corner, where
  they gave me a shot on the house, shut down.
- I earned my limits.
- I learned how to brew espresso without a machine.
  It worked like a dream!
- A Burma-born poet visited me. He got me wrong. On
  both counts. It was *Laizastrasse*, not *Leiserstrasse*.
  My number wasn't tango, tango, stereo, mirror, black,
  copper, yoko, tango, bread. It was tango, tango, stereo,
  mirror, black, copper, yoko, tango, bread, butter.
  No lift to my flat. Sorry.
- Earth filled her lap with sorrows of her own.
- I met a woman Genghis Khan. She read everything in
  Russian. I sold her to Gagarin.
- Some loft beds can be too lofty. Someone got turned off
  on the way up.
- Horror. In the month of September. The bananas I'd
  been eating every morning were conflict-soiled.
- I lost V, the glove for my left. V was thirteen-winters old
  On the way to look for her, I lost her identical twin, O, the
  glove for my right. O was only a couple of weeks old.

- The voice spoke to me, 'Accept Him as your Lord and Saviour. Instead of dying gradually you will move from glory to glory.'
- Professor Risotto, my neighbour's cat, died. What's her name? My neighbour's?
- *Literary Freud* I borrowed from the Library of Fine Arts but never read went missing. Fortnight. Overdue. I found it later inside *Macbeth: Psychological Shakespeare.*
- I was ready to be old.
- I wasn't.

ကော်ပတာ

ဟိလင်းအတွက်

နိုင်ငံခြားသွားဖို့ ဇာတာပါသူတိုင်း လေယာဉ်စီးကြရမှာပဲ ကော်ပတာကတော့ ကိုထူးမှ ကော်ပတာဆိုတာ ပျံတက်ဖို့ အရှိန်မလိုတဲ့အတွက် ဘီးမလို ဘီးမလိုတဲ့အတွက် ကွင်းမလို ဒေါင်လိုက်ကြီးတက် ဒေါင်လိုက်တက်ကြီးဆင်း

လေယာဉ်ပေါ်မှာ လေယာဉ်မယ်တွေ ဖိုလ်ကျတာ ခံရပေမဲ့ ကော်ပတာမယ် ဆိုတာမရှိ ရှိရင်လည်း သူ့ကို လုပ်ချင်တာလုပ် ကော်ပတာ ခရီးသည်ဆိုတာ ချက်အင်တို့ လုံခြုံရေးတို့ ဖြတ်နေစရာမလို နိုင်ငံကူးလက်မှတ်တို့ ဘော့ဒ်ဒင်းပက်စ်တို့ ပြနေစရာမလို

ကော်ပတာခရီးသည်ဟာ အဝတ်တထည်ကိုယ်တခု ပေ့ါပေါ့ပါးပါး ကော်ပတာထဲမှာ လူတန်းစားတစ်ရပ်ပဲ ရှိကယ် — အကက်ကနဲး ကော်ပတာပေါ်တက်ဖို့ တန်းစီစောင့်စရာ မလို ကော်ပတာ မထွက်ခင် မဆိုက်ခင် ခါးပတ် ပတ် ထိုင်ခုံ မတ် ဆိုတဲ့ လက်ချာတွေ နားထောင်နေစရာမလို

လေဆိပ်ဝေးရင် လမ်းမှာ ယာဉ်ကြောကျပ်နေရင် လေဆိပ်ကို သွားတဲ့အချိန်က လေယာဉ်စီးရချိန်ထက် ပိုကြာတတ်တယ်

ကိုယ့်လူ ပါပါ မပါပါ လယောဉ်ခရီးစဉ်ရှိန်မှောပဲ

Copter

for Han Lynn

Those who were born under the star of exile will experience a flight or two. For a taste of copter you've got to be super lucky. Copter doesn't need take-off speed. It doesn't need wheels and runway. Vertical ascension. That means vertical landing!

On an airplane, you are subject to a stewardesses' whim. There is no such thing as a copter stewardess. If there's a hostess on a copter, she is all yours. Copter passengers don't have to go through check-in or security. They don't have to carry passports or boarding papers.

Copter people are light travelers. There's only one class on copter—business. You don't need to line up to board a copter. On a copter, you're not subject to lectures about the benefits of buckling up or keeping your back straight during the flight.

If the airport is far, or when there's a traffic jam on the way to the airport, you'll be wasting your time travelling towards the airplane, rather than spending your time enjoying the flight.

With or without you, an airplane is set for a destination.

လေယာဉ်ဆိုတာ အတောင်တပ်ထားတဲ့ ဘုံအိမ်သာ

ကော်ပတာကတော့ ကံကြီးရှင်အတွက်

အိပ်ယာထဲ အေးဆေးနပ်နေ

အိမ်ခေါင်မိုးပေါ် ဆင်းလာမယ်

An airplane is a public toilet with wings.

Copter is for the exceptionally talented.

Just lay back and relax.

There'll be an airlift on your roof.

I ain't flying nowhere

Sorry, but I am busy. I am working on a new project. A
prototype man-fish, swim-talk, to be installed in a thank-tink.
The type that eats sultriness.

Are you in a hurry? Go ahead.

Your river is silted. Your beach needs nourishment. Your reef
gold must be sifted. Your paradigm shifted. Mercury you no
longer use. You simply get mercurial.

I will catch up with you later. I really mean real.

I will play the invisible theremin. I will finger thin air.

I will meditate until I levitate. I will eyeball the void until the
void blinks and blushes.

I will shadow Jan Hendrik Leopold,

I will sit very very still and travel.

Celebrations

Over here we celebrate absolutely everything, every single day. Everyday is someone's birthday or funeral. Every other day is an anniversary of a massacre or wedding. We celebrate every week when we delouse ourselves by rubbing our shaven heads with lime. Every three months, when we deworm our stomachs with papaya seeds. We celebrate the spiritual power of our polluted air. We celebrate plastic in our rivers. We celebrate the lives of spiders by frying them for food. We celebrate snakes by skinning them into jerky. Sex, real or imagined, is the celebration of the body's arousal. Orgasm is a celebration of body's contented closure. We celebrate celibacy. We celebrate and are humbled when rapists apologize. We feast with plenty of *arak* when a mother manages to rent her womb or sell her child. On the occasions of the funerals of poets who died from excessive drinking, we toast rice wine over their graves and get piss-drunk. When there's nothing to celebrate we celebrate for nothing, with nothing. All day long every single day of the year we smile and say to each other "How are you today? Have you eaten?" and "Sleep well." before bed. Come morning, we say "Have you eaten?" to celebrate the day, for we are still here.

ဝက်

အလှမယ်ပြိုင်ပွဲဝင် ဝက်မတစ်ကောင်လို ကိုယ်လေးလက်ဝင် လ ဟာ
သူ့ကျောရိုးကို ထင်းရှူးပင်နဲ့ ပွတ်ပြီး အသားဖြေဖို့ ကောင်းကင်က ဆင်းလာတယ်

မြင်းတွေကို အိပ်မက် မက်ရင် ခရီးဝေးသွားရကိန်းရှိတယ်   မြင်းတပ်နဲ့
သိမ်းပိုက်ထားတွဲ့မြို့မှာ နေဖူးရင် ငါပြောတာ မင်း သဘောပေါက်လိမ့်မယ်

ဝက်တွေကို အိပ်မက် မက်ရင် အပြောင်းအရွှေ့မရှိဘူး   ငါ ငယ်ငယ်က
အိမ်နောက်ဖေးခြံမှာ မြင်း မပြောနဲ့ မြင်းပုံတောင် မဆန့်

အမေက ဝက်မွေးတယ်   ဝက်ဆိုတာ ထွက်ရပ်ပေါက် မြင်းပုံတွေ
မြင်းပုံကို ဝက်လို တက်စီးလို့မရ

ငါဟာ မြင်းပုံကို ကုန်းနှီးမပါပဲ စီးပြီး တော်လှန်ရေးတွေကို နှိမ်နင်းခဲ့

ဝက်ထီး တစ်ကောင်ဒေးသင်းတိုင်း ကမ္ဘာပျက်တော့တာပဲ   ဝက်ဒေးစ္စတွေ
လိမ့်သွား   သွေးတွေ သွေးတွေ ရဲနေရဲ့

ငါ သိခဲ့တဲ့ ဆရာဆိုလို့ ဝက်ဒေးသင်းတဲ့ဆရာပဲ ရှိတယ်

မြင်းခွာသံ ကြားတိုင်း ငါ ရင်တုန်ပန်းတုန် ဖြစ်တုန်း   ရာနဲ့ချီတဲ့ မြင်းခွာတွေ
မျက်ရည်တောင်ကြားစစ်ပွဲက တဝှီးကားသံတွေလို တဝုန်းဝုန်း တဂျိုးဂျိုး

ကမ္ဘာပျက်ပြီးနောက် မြင်းပုံတွေပဲ ကျန်ရစ်နေခဲ့မယ်ဆိုပဲ

သိပ်တော့ မသေချာဘူး ထင်တယ်

Swine

Like a pageant sow the pregnant moon has lowered herself
to rub her spine against a pine limb.

If you dream of horses you will need to travel far. If you are
in a town under a cavalry siege, your dreams will be equine.

If you dream of pigs you will remain where you are. The back
garden of my childhood home was too small for a horse.

It was a pigpen. Pigs are enlightened winged horses. You don't
mount a Pegasus the way you mount a pig.

I rode bareback, I rode out all the revolutions.

Each time a young swine was castrated, all hell broke loose.
When balls rolled, blood went everywhere.

The only Master I got to know was the young Master whose
speciality was swine sterilization.

Hooves still ruffle my feathers—hundreds of hooves on gravel
roar like tanks rolling at the Valley of Tears Battle.

In the post-apocalyptic world,
only winged horses shall remain.

I am not so sure about that.

Chairs

§   The only chair they had in antiquity was the throne,
the most uncomfortable of stools, the jewel-studded unmovable,
the gentlest four-legged in history.

§   All cars are chairs on wheels, but not all wheelchairs are
cars. An average chair can tell you that charity always begins with
a chair. Radical chairs kill and get killed fighting for charism.
Romantic chairs think they are cherries. Academic chairs make
their living trying to prove the correlation between characins and
chairs.

§   The most boorish chairs are bureaucratic leather and
restless revolving chairs. The mass-produced ubiquitous type.
They love to roll with business jackets hung over their back.

§   Law of Chair

   – Every chair wants to sit at the top of the table.
   – Every chair wants to be a throne.
   – Every chair aspires to be at the highest place
     in the chapel.
   – Every chair prays to become the seat of god,
     the cathedral.

§   It's offensive to offer "a seat" to a visiting chair.
No chair wants to be addressed as a seat—a seat is just
a place for your buttocks.

§   Invisible air chairs are not made of air; they are
transparent plastic. The air that you must breathe does not
have the chair quality to support your ass. Invisible chairs are
proud of this piece of information.

§   Suicide by hanging is accomplished when a chair under
your feet is kicked away. No chair, however, will acknowledge
that no monarch has ever hanged himself by kicking off his
throne, the chair of all chairs.

§   Studies have shown that the design of a porcelain
throne is far from optimal for people's health. You are better
off on a squat commode—just as nature intended.

Funeral for an elephant

How many pallbearers does it take to shoulder an elephant's casket? How many teak planks are needed for an elephantine coffin? How many craftsmen? How many gallons of paint and polish? How many tons of long nails with textured heads?

Will they attach two pairs of gigantic trousers to the humongous coffin for the elephant's legs, and three holes in the front for the trunk and tusks? Should the casket be draped in Indonesian batik or a national flag? Eloquent eulogies have been penned. The top florists have been commissioned to come forward with fancy sympathy flowers and designer wreaths.

Perhaps an elephant is heavier dead? When an elephant dies, everybody's on edge. Even the ivory poachers send condolences. Security is at an all-time high. The rumor mill is in overdrive— radicals will highjack the casket and turn the funeral into a protest. All the tribal leaders will be there. They'll need six-deck cranes to lower the box into a grave the size of Lesotho. A 21-gun salute for such a mammoth figure may be too low-key, too ungenerous.

Of course the embalmers want the elephant.
'Keep it in a mausoleum. It's good for tourism.' they insist.

Lucky for us, the funeral director says, the elephant must rest.

'After all it wasn't a white elephant.'

Bullets are dangerous

Not least of which because they contain lead.

Lead is a heavy metal. A well documented environmental poison.

For contraception, Roman prostitutes ate *sapa*, lead sugar. The hairfall, toothfall and downfall of Queen Elizabeth I is attributed to a lead cosmetic she layered on her face. A seventeenth-century Burmese monarch loved to pour molten lead down the throats of captured pretenders to the throne, who would have done the same to him, had they succeeded.

Lead is nineteenth-century polonium. Once in the body, lead disrupts the function of δ-aminolevulinic acid dehydratase enzyme. Anything from headaches and sleeplessness to hallucinations, depression, fits and coma. Lead in the blood will corrode your skin, blacken your teeth, and bleed your gums blue. The black puke it produces will burn your gullet.

Bullets are dangerous. Especially when they are fired into a body at high velocity.

The difference between velocity and speed is—

velocity knows where it's going.

It ensures instant death.

ရှိမန်းတစ် စစ်စစ် ချောချောလေး

အလုပ်လုပ်ရခြင်းရဲ့ ပျော်ရွှင်ဖွယ်ရာနဲ့ ဝမ်းနည်းဖွယ်ရာ စာအုပ် သုတေသနပြုရင်း သန္ဓေကောင်းလာတဲ့ ကလေး သူမွေးတဲ့နေ့မှာ အိမ်နားက ထန်းပင်တစ်ပင်ကို မိုးကြီးပစ်တယ် ကျိုးတွေအာတယ် စားသုံးဆီဈေး ထူးထူးကဲကဲကျတယ်

အဲဒီစာအုပ်လား ပြိုင်ဖက်တစ်ယောက်က အရင်ဦးအောင်ရေးပြီး ထုတ်ဝေလိုက်တာ ရွာကျော် သွားတယ် ပင်လယ်နက် ရေပြင်ပေါ်မှာ ပက်လက်မျောရင်း ဆေးပြင်း လိပ်ခဲ့ရတဲ့ အရသာကို စည်းသွပ်မူး သွပ် ရောင်းမယ်ကြီတော့ ရင်းနှီးမြှုပ်နှံမှ ဥပဒေသစံနဲ့ ငြိနေတယ်

ဘယ်လောက်ရရ မရောင်းဘူးပြောရင်း ဈေးကောင်းပေးမဲ့သူကို မျှော်နေမိ မျှော်ပြဆန်တောင်းတွေကို သနားပြီး မျှော်က လိုက် က ပေးရတာတွေ ပျားလွန်းလာတော့ ခုတလော ကိုယ့်မြီးရှောင့်ရှိုးကို ကိုယ် မကြာမကြာ စမ်းမိနေတယ်

မိအေး နှစ်ခါနာထားတာတောင် ကောင်းမှန်းသိ သာအိ တစိုစို လုပ်ချင်တုန်း 'အဂတိတရားလေးပါး' ဆိုတဲ့ ခေါင်းစဉ်နဲ့ သူပြုစုခဲ့တဲ့ ပါရဂူစာတမ်းရဲ့ အနှစ်ချုပ်က 'ရှင်ကြီးဝမ်းလည်း နံတယ် ရှင်ငယ်ဝမ်းလည်း နံတယ်' ဆိုပဲ

The romanticism purist

He was conceived the moment the idea for the book *Joys and Sorrows of Work* hit his spermy parents. On the morning of his birth, a series of auspicious dillies were observed—a toddy palm in the neighbourhood was struck by lightning, crows were crowing, the price of cooking oil went down inexplicably.

What of the book? A rival published it first and went on to claim the Nobel Memorial Prize in Economic Sciences. His own business scheme—to can the luxury of back floating while smoking a Havana on the Black Sea—never took off. It is above the New Investment Law.

With his eyes trained on prospective bidders, he swears he'll never sell out. As he has far too often played monkey in pity of the monkey handlers who beg for rice in the name of monkey welfare, he is now in the habit of feeling his rear end to see if a tail has already sprouted.

On one cheek he acts like Angelina who's had it twice and grieves beyond solace. On the other, he acts like Brad who never gets it enough. In his PhD dissertation titled "The Four Forms of Graft" he has arrived at this conclusion: the Almighty Chaos' butt drool is as shitty as the lesser Apollo's.

ဒုတ်ထိုးအိုးပေါက် ဘယ်လောက်ပဲ တင်းထားတင်းထား လာလာဂိုပြရင် ပျော့ကျ
သွားတတ်မဲ့ မိမိကြောင့် ဘဝပျက်ခဲ့ဖူးသူတွေ တဦးချင်း တယောက်ချင်းစီကို
ရှာရှိးကိုးပေါက်ပတ်ပြီး အုန်းပွဲဝှက်ပြောပွဲနဲ့ လိုက်လံကန်တော့ တောင်းပန်ဖို့
အစီအစဉ် ရှိတယ်

စက်ရုပ်တွေအတွက်တော့ အနာဂတ်က လှတယ် ဒွါဒသမအကြိမ်မြောက်
ဆက်တိုက် ရွေးကောက်တင်မြှောက်တာ ခံယူပြီးရင် အငြိမ်းစားယူမယ်

He may be as hardy as a baseball bat that can bust your clay pot with ease. Yet he turns tender once he hears your tears rolling. One day he plans to fly around the globe to personally apologize to each of you whose life he has ruined.

He would do that in a typically Buddhist way, kowtowing with coconut-in-the-hands-of-bananas offering. The future is robust for robots. He will retire after you vote him in for the twentieth consecutive term.

ချင်းတွင်း [မြစ်ရဲ့ အမျက်]

ဆီလို အပေါက်ရှာတာမဟုတ် အပြည့်လွန်အိုးမို့
လျှံတက်တာ လင်ကောင်မပေါ်တဲ့ ဖိုက်က

ကျွှဲထိုးတာ မဟုတ် မြစ်နာကျလို့ လည်ချောင်းထဲက
ကြွပ်ကြွပ်အိတ်တွေကို ဝေ့ ဝေ့ နဲ့ ပြန်အန်ထုတ်တာ

ပဲမလှောင်ဘဲ ဆန်လှောင်တဲ့ သူတွေကို ရွှေး နိုပ်စက်
မူးမြစ်ထင်သူတွေကို အမောက်ထောင်ပြ လမ်းဘေး

ချိုးပါနေတဲ့ နိုင်ငံတော်ကို မေးငေါ့ မယ်ဘော်က ကဲက
တွေထက် ကဲပြတာ သူမ အန်ဖတ်တွေ ရေဘေး

အလှူခံခွက်တွေ ပြည့်တဲ့အထိ ပြက္ခဒိန်ကြည့်ပြီးမှ
ရာသီလာရမှာလား မိုးခေါင်ရင်ခေါင် မိုးမခေါင်ရင်

ရေကြီးမှာပဲ သူမကြောင့် ဒေသခံကဗျာဆရာတွေ
မြစ်ရေနဲ့ မျက်ရည် မသဲကွဲတော့တာ

The Chindwin [River rage]

She rises above the flood stage like an overfilled pot—a tight
pot that doesn't leak.

Hiccupping like a soon-to-be single mother, she will puke
back into your face all the plastic and rubber you've forced
into her throat. She belches stale draft. She is a river—hanging
on a river hangover.

Rice hoarders will be whipped. Split bean hoarders will be
spared. She will show what a dominatrix she is to those who
mistake the rivulet Mu for a river. Cross with the land, she
will piss on the road's shoulder.

Her refuse will fill disaster relief bowls. For her monthly does
she have to know the day of the calendar month? If there's no
bloody drought there will be a bloody deluge.

Local poets no longer make a distinction between
[river water] and [tear].

And now, how will you unfuck her?

after "Spelling Rhyme" by the Venerable Ashin Tikki Eaindra

- Advertisement, or announcement? Occupy, or squat?
  Right it up correctly, for the write effect.
- Your sleep-talk swells every night. If I'd waited up, I'd have
  been late, you bastard!
- Kicking the rattan ball, or hauling water? The audience is
  always there. Add hominem ad hominem.
- During the training session of division-level candidates,
  you get a correct when your waste is high.
- Collect dry twigs for firewood only when you find them
  burned out over the great gorge.
- Anniversary in the midfield of a minefield? Midday mustn't
  be separated.
- Bed, betel, left or right. Households aren't two words.
- The oath and the destiny aren't the same. Know their difference.
- Shrimps, crabs, or numerals? Keep the record straight.
- Sunning something out there? Wrap it up in a banana leaf.
  Once a fistful of rice is eaten from him, you must serve him
  all your life.
- To admire a stupa? To look out for danger? You can only anticipate.
- Don't kowtow at a Queen for a gilded pagoda.
- Scratch, or doodle, bitter-sweet love? Have loving-kindness for all.
- Value your elders. Lower yourself in front of them.
- Frying and boiling entail cooking. Fix your glitch if it's broken.
- Spread the rice seedlings fairly and squarely in the wet field.
  Seal anything that droops or snoops.
- Seen that, done it? There, a deference. Box the ointment
  immediately and burp, "Belch!"

On the eve of nuclear holocaust

All I could think of is sex, sex, sex.

At the end of all my nerves, what does it feel to be human?

The bathing beach is full of women, half-naked. They all look young, and stout. The able-bodied women would be enlisted in war times. Their children will go to war too, replacing their soon-to-be-dead parents.

Mr. Ashbery turned ninety the other day. What must have he endured, or enjoyed?

Some houses are still lit even in the blackout.

Some people are aroused by peril.

I look at myself in the mirror. In the half-light, the reflection of my wrinkly dotage

fully erect, and dripping wet.

နေ့ထူးနေ့မြတ်

မိုးရာသီဆိုပေမဲ့
တိမ်ကင်းစင်ပြီး နေသာတဲ့နေ့
တခြားနေ့တွေထက် ဘာမှမထူးပေမဲ့
တခြားနေ့တွေထက် ရာသီဥတု ပိုကောင်းတယ်
လပြည့်ကျော်တစ်ရက်နေ့
ဘာ၏တွေ မဝိတ်ဘူး

ဒီနေ့နဲ့ပတ်သက်ပြီး နား‌လည်မှုအလွဲတွေ အများကြီး
ပေးဆပ်ခဲ့တာနဲ့ ပြန်ရခဲ့တာ
ချိန်ခွင်လျှာ တဖက်စောင်းနင်း
အဲဒီလို တွက်ကြတဲ့သူချည်း

အရှုံးတွေဟာ တကယ်မရှုံး
အလွဲတွေက အမှန်တွေလည်းဖြစ်နိုင်တယ်
သူတို့ဟာ ကြေကွဲမှုကို တစစီဖွတ်ပြီး
တက်တက်ကြွကြွ ပြန်တပ်လိုက်ကြတယ်

အဲဒီနေ့က ငါ ဘာလုပ်နေခဲ့လဲ
ဒီတခါတော့
ဒီမေးခွန်းကို
ငါ ဖြေချင်လဲ့ရတယ် မဖြေချင်လဲ့ရတယ်

A very special day

It's a monsoon. The sun is out. The sky is blue.

But for the better weather, today is no different from any other monsoon day. Today is the first waning day of the moon. No bank holiday.

There have been several misunderstandings surrounding today in history. What has been sacrificed? To what end?

Crazy is not nearly insane. Spot on is off the mark.

The right pan on the scales of justice careens with nothingness.

They have disassembled grief and, in earnest, reassembled it.

What was I doing that day?

Today, I am no longer obliged to answer that question.

A grand tragedy on a grain of rice

High above the walls of the four seasons, the multiverses
are expanding, and parallel. The milkyway, the star-studded
white dress, hangs over the moon's crescent.

Ram, bull, twins, crab, lion, virgin, scales, scorpion, archer,
goat, water bearer, fish . . .

What mundane names for celestial particles! Are mutable
signs compatible with fixed signs? Would constellations
faraway know why? Am I in the void of a lunar cycle?

Who am I to relate myself to stellar fate?
All the suns burn a slow death. All the galaxies shift their
alignment. Astrologers are no mensches.

In the finer scheme of things

—you would have never left.

I've lived to learn in life's hard school

That each time I breathe I eat a large hole in the earth.

I am the filthiest of the great unwashed.

I am the cause of the planet's heartburn.

If you fancy *soixante-neuf,* you will get cancer of the tongue.

I am the deadly, winking, sniggering, snuggling, chromium-plated, scent-impregnated, luminous, quivering, giggling, fruit-flavoured, mincing, ice-covered heap of love.

I am they. I am entirely entwined.

You isn't them.

Have I invented veganism? My right hand doesn't know my left is in the till.

I lead a slow life in a fast nation. Everything that leaks or explodes bears traces of my action.

When I am not loitering at the cockfight—

I leave my cattle grazing your grass.

The Thingyan prophecy for the Buddhist Year 1379

Banuraja, the Sun King, wielding an axe in one hand and
a sickle in the other, in an equipage the colour of a bathing
conch shell, rides the Lord of Bovines. He shall rise from the
Thursday Pole, in the southeast corner, and descend towards
the Tuesday Pole, in the west.

The goddess Praukkadevi, tasked with the upkeep of the
decapitated head of the Brahma Ahsi over the past year,
passes the head to the goddess Rathakadevi, whose time
has come.

Sitting on her heels, with hands outstretched, Rathakadevi
receives the bloody head.

Meanwhile, in her cumulus gilt chamber, the goddess
Nandadevi anticipates Thagyamin, the Celestial Chief,
in a rococo dress of white, red, green, blue and yellow silk.

All planets in space, all things considered, in the
forthcoming Myanmar Buddhist year of 1379,

– Early and mid monsoon will be bad. Late monsoon
   will be good.
– Merit-making projects, construction of pagodas, stupas,
   temples and lakes, abound.

- An evil sarong-wearing lady will ruin many a decent
  sarong-wearing lady.
- Four-legged creatures, especially cows and water buffalos,
  are in grave danger.
- Nations, big and small, shall be gripped with a fear of
  unknown unknowns.
- Rare is silk, for silk is rare.

Twelve art project proposals in Ai Weiwei-like proportions

– *Walled*: A life-sized Great Wall of China, made of gold LEGO bricks, to be installed around the White House for the occasion of the 4th of July; in the event that LEGO declines to supply bricks for the project, copies of *What Happened*" by Hillary Clinton will be used as bricks

– *Saffron Skies*: Saffron shrouds to be placed over Beijing, London, Yangon, Brussels and Berlin, each giant shroud a patchwork of used saffron robes culled from a million monks in Myanmar; this summer installation is set for nine days, hinting at the nine qualities of the Lord Buddha

– *Selfie King in the Heavenly Palace*: Taking a selfie from Tiangong-1 space station against the backdrop of the entire population of China—Chinese citizens, including those from Taiwan, Hong Kong and Macau, are requested to come out for the occasion and look up at the artist on Tiangong-1 for a selfie, after which the artist will return to earth to meet individually with the participants for one-on-one selfies; an estimated 1.3 billion selfies with the artist are to be displayed in a purpose-built museum modelled after Ai Weiwei's head; the museum will be named Heavenly Palace [*Tiangong*]

– *Project 42*: Out of forty-three Fabergé eggs left in the world, forty-two are to be smashed with a baseball bat in Yankee Stadium, both the hitter (the artist) and the pitcher (Lady Gaga or Beyonce, to be confirmed), will be nude and televised live; '42' alludes to the meaning of life

– *Mechanical Cicadas*: The Eiffel Tower is to be covered in a colony of 1,789,000,000 hand-wound mechanical cicadas that will drone for refugees for 1789 hours; the installation can be moved to landmarks all around the world

– *Troll Tongue Tied*: Breaking off the Troll Tongue [Trolltunga, Norway], and replacing it with a hyper-realistic rubber-plastic hybrid tongue for a spring day display

– *Terracotta Ai-me (Greater China)*: A total of 2,285,000 Ai Weiwei statues fashioned after China's Terracotta soldiers to be installed on Tiananmen Square for the occasion of China's PLA Day, the number 2,285,000 being the size of the twenty-first century Greater China Armed Forces

– *Slant-1*: The Fallingwater at Mill Run, Pennsylvania, to be tilted 45 degrees to the right; permanent installation

– *Slant-2*: The Jade Pagoda in Mandalay, Myanmar, to be tilted 45 degrees to the east; permanent installation

– *Worldwide Womb*: A hyper-realistic larger-than-life womb of a nine-month pregnant woman, complete with chemically reproduced amniotic fluid; any volunteer who would like to coil up naked in the womb in the foetal position for a minimum duration of nine hours will be supplied with an oxygen mask and a feeding tube; her situation will be constantly monitored and televised; a couple or a family of three can also volunteer to be in the womb to simulate twins or triplets, volunteers are free to choose their preferred way out, pushing strenuously through a rubber vagina or Caesarean section; permanent installation

– *Pilgrim Whale-99*: A 99-meter blimp, the shape of a blue whale, to kiss the banana bud of the 99-meter tall Shwedagon Pagoda, for the Double Ninth Festival

– *Seediness-neediness*: One million infinitesimal porcelain poppy seeds in the eye of an average-sized needle, to be eyed by up to ten thousand people at a time using a gigantic clinical microscope the size of the World Trade Center in New York City; permanent installation

How to cheat fate for a true marriage

May the two clay pots touch
May the two cotton strings entangle!

Clay pots at the ready, gild one gold, the other silver.

Glue his portrait to the gold, yours to the silver.

Gold pot for the flowers of your day of the week.
Silver for the flowers of his day of the week.
If you are Sunday's daughter plant 6 coconut flowers
in the gold.
For Friday's son, place 21 frangipani blooms in the silver.

The rest is here:
               – 15 monkey face orchids for Monday.
               – 12 hooker's lips for Tuesday.
               – 13 naked men orchids for Wednesday.
               – 19 corpse flowers for Thursday.
               – 21 dancing girls for Saturday.

Right under the nose of your house Buddha,
put the two clay pots together on a table.

May the two clay pots touch!
May the two cotton strings entangle!

နိုင်ငံရေးနဲ့ ပြိုခြင်း

သူမ လည်ချောင်းထဲ နင်နေတဲ့ ငါ့ကဗျာကို ခြေမနဲ့ ကော်ထုတ်လိုက်ပြီး
မျက်ရည်ပေါက်ကြီးငယ်ကို စာလုံးသစ်တစ်လုံးနဲ့ အစားထိုးလိုက်တယ်

အထက်ဆင်မပါတဲ့ သူမရဲ့ ထဘီအနားဟာ နွေထနောင်း ဆောင်းမန်ကျည်း
အဲဒီနွေက မိုးမရွာဘူး ရေမကြီးဘူး – အသေးစိပ်တွေ အရေးမကြီးဘူး

အခန်းထောင့်က သုံးချောင်းထောက် သစ်သားစင်ပေါ်က စစ်ကိုင်းအိုးလေးမှာ
အရင်အိမ်ရှင် ထိုးတို့ထားခဲ့တဲ့ 'အရဟံ' ဟာ သေးသေးတင်ပြွတ် ရကောက်

ပျက်ပြီး 'အ ဟ' ဖြစ်နေပြီ သစ်ပင်မြင့်မြင့် ဖြစ်ခဲ့လို့ လေတိုက် တော်တော်ခံခဲ့ရတဲ့
သစ်မာသားနဲ့ဆောက်ထားတဲ့ ပျဉ်ထောင်အိမ်လေးတစ်လုံးမှာ သူမနဲ့ငါ ညားတယ်

စပါးတွေနဲ့ လေးလံပြီး အမြဲဦးညွတ်ရိုကျိုး သလိုဖြစ်နေခဲ့တဲ့ စပါးနဲ့က
ဆန်နဲ့ သူမကို ငါ ထမင်းချက်ကျွေးတယ် ငါ ပြောချင်တာက အိမ်အကြောင်း

ကျွေဆန်အကြောင်းမဟုတ် ငါ ပြောနေတာက သူမလည်ပင်းထဲ နင်နေတဲ့
ငါ့ ကဗျာအကြောင်း အဲဒီကဗျာမှာ စာကြောင်းတစ်ကြောင်းကို နှစ်ခါမထပ်ဘူး

အဲဒီကဗျာမှာ စာကြောင်းတစ်ကြောင်းကို နှစ်ခါမထပ်ဘူး

Upper black lining

I toe off the poem stuck in her throat. Teardrops big and small
will be replaced with a neologism.

The hem of her sarong I now cling to for life has no black lining
at the waistline. *Tanuang* provides shade in the summer.
Tamarind, a warm shelter in winter. It does't rain or pour—
details aren't important.

A scribble on the Sagaing clay pot resting on a wooden tripod
in the corner of the room reads PER   ION. Should it read

PERFECTION, the supreme quality of the Lord Buddha? The
scribble in lime must have been the work of a past tenant.

The stilt house in our wedlock is planked with timber from the
hardwood trees that used to compete in height in their effort to
gain better exposure to jungle sun.

White ants are everywhere. I cook her rice with large buffalo
grains that used to weigh down the whole paddy. That paddy is an
industrial zone today.

This is not about the stilt house. Not about the buffalo grains.
This is about the poem stuck in her throat. In that poem, there are
no two lines in refrain.

In that poem, there are no two lines in refrain.

Seasonal flu

When the vessel overladen with padauk logs sinks in the Ayavadi, the logs float upstream back to the northern jungles. People watch the scene—their mouth agape. Out of each gaping mouth rocks a brand-new chainsaw.

When water rises, water woes rise with water. When water recedes, water woes remain.

Tiger mosquitos prefer living rooms where graduation photos proudly hang on the walls.

Seasonal flu brings along with her the scent of seasonal flowers. Elegant is her gait as that of a she-elephant. The she-elephant is in the living room.

Personal hygiene is most vital for women who like islands are surrounded by water. No woman is an island. Avoid crowded places. If you must go south, do not touch any hardwood handrails in staircases.

Sleep tight.

Let tiger mosquitoes window-shop outside your mosquito net.

Amongst the world's marvellous marbles

I am the Diamond Marble. I am a cross between the bull's eye atop a
top and the screw that caps the fastest fan you can imagine. Each time
I wave my hand, lettuce flowers at my fingertips. I swap fake dolls for
pearl flakes. Fake pearl flakes for dope dolls. I man every highway
road in your land, every highway restaurant, every toddy palm
plantation, and every fuel station next to those highway restaurants.
The Internet you worship is my property. I am the Patron Saint of
your Party. I eat rabid dogs. I feed poisoned meat to your pet. The
way I squat-shit on a Western toilet, I sit above your government. It
was me who painted a toothbrush moustache on the national gallery
portrait of your favourite General. Listen up, Sonny! Unbeknownst
to you, your mother was one of my 18,000 fretwork footrests I
clubbed with sex. When you were a crawler, sick with anal scabies you
contracted from bathing at my charity well, your mother had to rush
you to my charity clinic, in one of my charity vehicles. For the sake of
your skin's hygiene, my sanction wiped out your filthy tribe. You grew
up half-baked, having been thrown into potboilers in the shambolic
public library I donated. I caused every episode of depression you
drowned in. I bottled every moonshine you drank.

I am *not* for profit.

They call me the Virtuous Circle—

I spin so fast history can't catch up, let alone blackmail me for a rest.

How to win friends and influence people

1. Pleasantries

The deeper the bow, the longer the conversation. Size him
up with a sneer! Faced with a solar stance, assume the most
unassuming posture, *shizentai*!

2. Augmented tofu pyramid delusions

Conceal your disarming tactics in intricate dance moves. Let
yourself float in free association. Let there be the Buddha's
Palm, Santa's Claws, Pankration Punch, Tumbling Fist, Flood
Fist, Mantis Fist, Ultimate Elbows, Organic Solidarity Hook,
Proud Nation's Knees, One-Finger Zen—*Si* for *Shi*.

3. A woodpecker sees the trees for the wood

Pay particular attention to his Extraordinary Meridians.
This will internalize the externalities. In the 31 Chambers of
Impermanence, up against the Five Ancestors' sword, splutter
pure colours of representational hyper-reality. Whizz a perfect
execution of Opium Optimum. Whirl through the pool of
bluebloods. When the wine is refilled, hold your half-empty
glass by the stem, shake it gently before you nose it.

4. Social elevator tantra mantra

Out of jacaranda into bull hoof,
  Out of bull hoof into cobra's saffron,
    Out of cobra's saffron into beautyleaf.

5. Avoid the guillotine choke

Never take a blood bath. Never make a blood oath. Never trust a blood brother. Never read a pillow book. Never fight the pillow fight.

Never use a pillow for a stepladder.

Sorry for saying fuck you

Yours is the most beautiful set of eyes I've ever set eyes on. May the sun never set on those eyes! I assure you, *you* in this context includes you and I, and their mirror images. It's not Brecht's *we*, which doesn't include us.

While you are in the habit each evening of taking a candlelit bath with your pet python, while you dye your hamster blue and dress him up like Amadeus, before feeding the blue Amadeus to the snake, while you tell me how wasteful I am with my penchant for licking quail eggs before I swallow them whole, how inane I am for attempting to rebuild our relationship, plank by plank, while on the high seas, you refuse to see the nature of the coldblooded predator even after seeing his victim, whose eyes were frozen beyond fear like thoroughly licked quail eggs, you complain incessantly about your sleep where nightmares as nightmarish as mine don't dwell, then you go on to whinge how irate you get by my *I love you* sleep-talk as you whip me up with a knout to demand the disambiguation of *you* in *I love you* . . .

Metaphors

They don't explain. They don't connect.

They don't say what they mean. They don't mean what they say.
They don't tell you the whole story. They make you imagine
them so you cannot imagine any other.

Much has been lost. *Much* has been lost.

In likeness. In precedence. In ranks. In files. In smiles. In frame.

Kidney is bean. Sunshine is lady. Chickpeas peck on peachicks.
Aren't they only doing their duty?

From love gaze to hate stare why is it that unfamiliar is always
sacrificed at the alter of overfamiliar?

If you candlelight moonlight, you might as well moonlight
candlelight. Sometimes, they are way off, you might as well take
a taxi to catch them.

Bastards! After gate-crashing your funeral, they don't return
your call.

When they finally ring a bell, you don't know where to place them. They have network problems. They are synthetic. They can't stand the cold. Even in the silt season, they don't yield.

Be careful with metaphors.

Whatever they give you with one hand, they take back with another.

The sky has collapsed

The King is dead.

The bereaved wear yellow. The future of His Majesty's Kingdom
as bleak as black.

Now how will His Majesty's weak-kneed subjects rise to their
feet to the mosaic photo display of His Majesty's remarkable
life in the cinema before the corporate commercials, before the
feature begins?

At 8 am and 6 pm every day, when the Royal Anthem is played
on all TV and radio stations, on government building speaker
systems, on public address systems in public transport and
public spaces, how will His Majesty's humble subjects, knowing
that His Majesty has passed, pause whatever they are doing,
raise their head high in regal pride, and stand at attention?

Even the Crown Prince himself requests time to mourn with
the people.

Before the new immortal is enthroned,

His Majesty's Kingdom will be anarchical.

အာလူး

နွယ်မြက်သစ်ပင်ဆေးဖက်ဝင် ဆိုသူများရဲ့ အသိအမှတ်ပြုခြင်း မခံရ
ကန်စွန်းဥကို အာလူးချို့လို့ခေါ်သူများနဲ့ သဟဇာတမဖြစ်
အာလူးသီးလို့ ခေါ်ရင် သူတမျိုးလုံးကို ကော်ဆဲသလို နာတတ်
ဘယ်သူကမှ အလုံးလိုက်မမြှိုနိုင် ဘာအကောင်မှ မပေါက်မယဲ့ ဥ
ကြက်သွန်နီထက် အခွံပါး သစ်ကြားသီးထက် အသည်းမာ
ဖရဲသီးလောက် မရွှမ်း သြဇာသီးလောက် မလန်း
သူ့တကိုယ်လုံးက မျက်စိတွေကို ကာဖို့ နေကာမျက်မှန်မရှိ
ဇော်ဒကာချက်ရာမှာ အခရာကုန်ကြမ်းတစ်ခု
သီးချိုန်တန်တာတွေ ပွင့်ချိုန်တန်တာတွေ နားမလည်ရှာ
ဆောင်းတွင်းမှာတောင် အလိုက်မသိ အညှောက်ပေါက်တတ်သူ
အဖွတ်ခံရရင် သူ့အရေပြားတွေ မဲလာပြီး မီးသွေးခဲကို အံတု
အပြွတ်ခံရရင် မူးပဲမတ်ပဲနဲ့အပြိုင် အရင်းနှုးချင်သူ
သူ့ကို ပါးပါးလှီးပြီး ဆီပူပွက်ပွက်ထဲ စိမ်ကြော်ရင်တောင်
ဆီပူကို သူ့ရင်ဘတ်ထဲ အကြာကြီး ထည့်သိမ်းထားတတ်သူ
သူ့ကို ဆုံထဲထည့်ထောင်းပြီး မွမွချေပစ်တာတောင်
ကာရာအိုကေရောက်ရင် ကမ္ဘာသစ်တေးကို အမြဲဆိုတတ်
ခြောက်ထောင့်ကြယ်အလံ ခရမ်းရောင်ပန်းများရဲ့ ဖခင်ကြီး
တောင်အမေရိကတိုက်ရဲ့ လူသိအများဆုံး တော်လှန်ရေးသမား
မြေအောက်လှုပ်ရှားသူဘဝတည်းက သားသတ်လွတ်စားခဲ့သူ

Aloo

Underappreciated by those to whom all herbs, plants, roots and tubers are medicinal, Aloo doesn't get along with those to whom every Yam is Sweet Potato. Calling him Spud is an insult to his race. He is an egg from which no hatchling will emerge. His skin is thinner than Onion's. His heart harder than Walnut's.

Aloo is not as succulent as Watermelon. Not as furtive as Custard Apple. No one can swallow him whole. No sunshade is cool enough for the eyes all over his body.

An indispensible ingredient for vodka, he has no sense of time and place. He will bloom when he likes, and where he likes. When you let him overwinter under your kitchen sink he will surprise you with Aloo sprouts.

When he is baked, his skin gets tanned—he will compete with the darkest of wood coal that bakes him. When he is boiled with others, he will try to outperform Lentils and Drumsticks in an endurance contest. Even if you slice him into thin film, and deep-fry him, he will be singing "The New World" at karaoke.

He is the undisputed original Hexagram, the Father of purple flowers, the most celebrated revolutionary from Latin America.

He has been a vegan since he was underground.

လေကြီးမိုးကြီး

မိဖုရားခေါင်ကြီးဖြစ်ဖို့ မရည်ရွယ်ခဲ့
နိုင်ငံရေး စိတ်ဝင်စားဖို့ နေနေသာသာ
ကလေးဘာသာဘာဝ ဖန်ခုန် ဇယ်တောက်သာ ပျော်မွေ့ခဲ့
ဖြစ်ပုံက လေကြမ်းတုန်း လှုန်းထားတဲ့ ထဘီကို
ပြေးအရုတ် လေကအရင် မ သွားတာ
အဲဒီထဘီ အင်းဝရွှေနန်းတော်ပြဿဒ အမြင့်ဆုံးမှာ သွားချိတ်
'ဘုန်းတော်ကြောင့် အင်မတန်ကြီးမြတ်မယ့်
မိန်းမရဲ့ ထဘီမို့ ပြဿဒနဲ့ ငြိကြောင်းပါ ဘုရား'
ဘကြီးလောက်ရှိတဲ့ ဘကြီးတော်က တော်ကောက်တာခံရ
ရွှေရင်သိမ်းသစ် ဆယ်ကျော်နှစ်မှာ မိဖုရားခေါင်ကြီး
နန်းမတော် မယ်နုဖြစ်လာ ဘကြီးတော်လက်ထက်
အောက်မြန်မာပြည် အင်္ဂလိပ်လက်အောက်ရောက်
ဒါကို မကြေလည်တဲ့ ဘကြီးတော်ညီ သာယာဝတီမင်းသားက
အာဏာသိမ်းတော့ မိဖုရားခေါင်ကြီး မယ်နုကို ရေနှစ်သတ်ခဲ့

ဒီနေ့ မိုးလေဝသ သတင်းအရ လေတိုက်နှုန်း ပြင်းမတဲ့
နိုင်ငံရေးအာဏာကို စိတ်မဝင်စားတဲ့ မချမ်းသာချင်တဲ့
ဟာမလေးတွေ

ညည်းတို့ အတွင်းခံတွေ ထဘီတွေ မြန်မြန် ရုတ်ထားကြ

Gust

She never wanted to be Queen Regnant. Forget politics, she
wasn't even into hopscotch. She was fond of flicking custard
apple seeds into a hole in the ground. What happened was this.
She'd hung her sarong out to dry on a gusty day. When the
wind started licking her sarong, she ran out to get it but it was
too late. Soon the whole Kingdom of Ava saw the sarong, blown
off by the gale, entangled at the top palace spire, flapping like
a royal banner. "Owing to your Majesty's Eminent Prowess,
the owner of this sarong must be extraordinarily blessed. She
must be made your Majesty's Queen Consort." Me Nu was just
a girl going through puberty when she was crowned Queen
Consort by Big Uncle King. After Lower Burma was annexed to
British India, the Prince of Thayawaddi, a brother of Big Uncle,
overthrew the King. No royal blood must be shed. The Royal
Executioners of Ava drowned the nineteen-year-old Queen
Consort in the Irrawaddy.

Attention, gals! Weather forecasts say it's going to be gusty
today. If you are not into power or money, hurry and remove
your undies and sarongs from the clotheslines!

Ceiling

During the transition, barbed wire was upgraded to razor wire.

The *Playgirl* cover boy into *Playboy* cover girl.

She screams new money without an orchestra.

She is not supposed to outperform her customers.

From the 100th floor you can see the whole city.

When the sky is clear, visibility is as good as the weather.

Lest you loose your showbiz sheen, don't let her stroke your
                              coat, or coke your vodka

Let me gainsay and grandstand;

For you, whom the gods wish to destroy,

they will first make you tender.

Lawns

for Yuval Noah Harari

From the Midwest to the Middle East, the rich eat lawns.

Polo and golf, the classiest of classy games, play out on lawns.

If you don't belong, lawns will yell at you,

"Piss off, you don't belong!"

Economic abs, military biceps and political glutes of nation states are reflected on government lawns.

Even a tiny patch of private turf demands land, tanks of water and backbreaking labour.

In exchange, lawns give you nothing.

Grass is for cattle.

Lawns

for Lords, and Lawmakers.

နိုင်ငံရေးသိပ္ပံ

ရေ ရေ ရေ လို့ တဆာဆာ တောင်းဆိုနေတဲ့ လျှာတွေ
အာဏာရှင် ဆေးလိပ်ပြာခွက် နှုတ်ခမ်းထူကို လျက်ပေးရပါများလွန်းလို့
ခြောက်သယောင်းနေကြ အဆုံးမရှိတဲ့
အုန်းဆိုကြိုးရဲ့အစကို သူတို့ မီးမြှိုက်လိုက်ကြပြီ

ဖုံးဆိံထဲမှာ အသက်ဓာတ်မရှိ   ဆေးလိပ်ပြာထဲမှာ ရေဓာတ်မရှိ
အတွင်းဒဏ်ရာတွေကို ဆေးမြီးတိုနဲ့ကုစားဖို့ သူတို့ ကြိုးစားခဲ့ကြတယ်
[မအောင်မြင်ဘူး]   ဆူနာမီဖြစ်တဲ့အတွက် ပင်လယ်ကို လိပ်ကြောက်မြီးနဲ့
ရိုက်ပြီးအပြစ်ပေးတယ် [ပင်လယ်ကနားမထောင်ဘူး]

ဒီမြေမှာ ထမင်းငတ်သေတဲ့ မသာမရှိဘူးလို့ သူတို့ ကြွေးကြော်နေကြတုန်း
သူတို့ရင်ဝယ်ပိုက်လေးတွေ အာဟာရချို့တဲ့ ပိန်လို့ဆုံးပါးသွားကြတယ်

ငါတို့ထဲကတချို့ကျ သမိုင်းတွေးတွေးကိုမှ ရွေးကြိုက်တယ်

တချို့ကျ မိုးခါးရေကြိုက်ပြီး တချို့ကျ မိုးခေါင်လို့ မောင်ခိုးတာလို့ ပြောတယ်

တန်ဆေးလွန်ဘေး ဆိုတာကို ထမင်းတလုပ် တုတ်တချက်စားရင်း

ငါတို့ သင်ကြားခဲ့ကြတယ်

Political science

A tongue that demands "Water! Water! Water!" is chapped.
from tonguing the thick lips of a totalitarian ashtray.

You may find life in a bombshell. There is no water in ash.
They redress their national internal bleeding with quacky
tincture. There's no cure for national internal bleeding.
To tame the tsunami they whip the ocean with a knout.
The ocean doesn't bother.

"On this land . . . ," Their slogan goes, " . . . there's no corpse
who died from starvation!" Every infant who heard that
has shrunk into a skin-on bones carcass.

Drought makes you think, thieve and thrive.

"Moderation is medicine, excess—poison," lectures a baton
blow on a citizen.

Some of us love flexural history.

Others make do with bitter rainwater.

The Ouroborous

It's no coincidence that snake venom is packed with its own counteragent.

Snakes are reptiles of repentance.

When a snake makes a slight humanlike mistake, a sin as it is known in the ophidian world, she will painfully shed her skin in penance.

When gripped with insurmountable guilt, she will swallow her own tail.

She'll stoically eat herself up in self-depreciation, until she forms the shape of a

perfect zero—

to go vanish into thin air.

No one wants to play with me

The school is sick with measles. Shall we hopscotch or skip rope? Shall we skip the skips?

Shall we miss school and play house for five years? Let's run around in the drizzle. Let's play floating figs, back-swimming along the downstream. Can you show me your shiny new marbles? I've got some apples.

You mustn't think outside the sandbox. You mustn't cheat. You mustn't invoke the head of our village boogeymen, your dead grandpa.

Little Zonja has lazy eyes. She never cries. You be her eye doctor. Her pupils see zigzag, periphery, and con. Her eyes are definitely off colour. That explains her depth perception problems.

Tiger, you look snazzy, holding a Kalashnikov.

Look at me,

I have an Uzi, from my big soldier brother!

Gallbladder

G-A-L-L-B-L-A-D-D-E-R?

What a dreadful sound from such a tiny hollowed body!

A thunder, bolted between liver and stomach, a bastard among better endowed entrails, a fish sauce hawker at a diamond auction.

A redundant tooth, at least, makes your smiles qualitatively more attractive.

Gallbladder doesn't hold a heart.

Don't fret. Your insides look infinitely sweeter without

T-H-A-T   G-O-D   D-A-M-N-E-D

G-A-L-L-B-L-A-D-D-E-R!

From the first kick to the final whistle

Cockroach's been had!
Cockroach's been beheaded!

It all started when we tossed around with our feet our war
trophy, the head of our enemy king.

Had the enemy king been a real cockroach,

he would have survived the decapitation, and died from
humiliation.

Since then, all our foes have been overplaying pain

mainly to induce free tickets.

A union of woke anonymous

[a]

Grit in my rice, piss in my rain
Sewage in my curry, sugar in my blood
I held out for sixty-four years
I would have survived the Avici hell.

[b]

Twenty years just for operating a book circle.
The first ten years, with needles turned upward under my naked
soles, they made me squat on my toes, with my hands extended.
They called it "motorcycle." For the next ten years my legs were in
a concrete cast. I was rotting bottom-up. They told my family I'd
died from a heart attack.

[c]

When I was eight, I was forced to marry that bastard. He died from
food poisoning the first night. They found me guilty of mariticide.
My village stoned me to death.

[d]

I refused to thank the land grabber who had returned me some
of my ancestral lands. He shot me in the head.

[e]

When I was a chicken, I saw my mother being roasted in a
microwave oven. When I came home to roost one evening,
I was run over by a bicycle.

[f]

I was signing a petition for the better treatment of laboratory
mice on my mobile device when I had a car accident.

[a, b, c, d, e, f together]

To all our living comrades,
Shall we raise our glasses
Shall we not clink
Let's drink in silence!

Variations on the soul

§   **shade**

Fluid, and mutable.

Soul springs forth from where the sun sets. She floats eastwards on the arch of heaven into the Ocean of Life where the sun rises. Then she travels again upstream on the subterranean River of Death.

Shade has no shape.
Shade has no colour.
Shade casts no shadow.

Shade dances an intricate dance.

§   **leaf**

Utterly uncontainable.

This precarious peach leaf will whoosh up towards the welkin, when the tree is gently shaken.

She will play catch and release. She will throw flaming bras at you. You need her, and she needs you—

even if she pretends not to.

§ **breath**

A cool draft encased in a skull, soul never sated.
Once she's let out, she stays out.
She will remain eternally incorporeal.

No more fixation than pillow attachment.
No less lethal than Agent Orange.

No Ajatar.
No Basilisk.
No Chukwa.

§ **data**

Speediest of all souls. *Amortal*, but not immortal.

For even time warps at the speed of light.

Unrelated to spirit. Self and soul think pure numbers.

They lead a life of their own.
It rains o's and 1's between 1 and 0.
Anima mundi of algorithms—

disconnection means death.

They lead a life of their own.

It rains o's and 1's

between 0 and 1.

§   **butterfly**

Lyrical-cyclical.

Life in a perpetual loop of birth, decay, death and rebirth.

Soul has come a long way since her caterpillar life.

She will flirt and flutter, especially when she negotiates a difficult landing

in the womb

of a soon-to-be-conceived teenage girl.

I voted for irony

A sardonic one at that.

Haven't I already terrorized your image-nation between
iconoclastic and romantic notions? I stopped believing in
fictions long ago.

The philistine has decapitated the aesthete. With a blunt
bamboo knife.

There's no sense when guns spell money. When guns spill
money correctly, poetry loses currency. There's no consolation
in conventional wisdom. There's no comfort in sedentary life.

I salute you. You, the deprived and the depraved, you who
drool barbaric bardic mannerism! You who was raped at
thirteen, learned forgiveness, but never learned to write.
I am done with transmuting daily glooms into lines of love
and death. Down with censorship. Down with dramas.

I don't want to work language from the outside. Like a fresh
corpse dissolved in language, I want my tongue dissolved in
lye. But what lye?

အမဲသား

သက်ကြီးစကား သက်ငယ်နားထဲက မိုးမျှော်လွန်ဆွဲပွဲအပြီးမှာ

နွားပေါက်လေးတွေ မိုးရွာသလို ရွာချတယ် မြေသင်းနဲ့ မရဘူး

အုတ် ဘိလပ်မြေ ပြိုကျသံ ကြက်တွန်သံလို မှန်မှန် ကြားနေရ

နကျယ်အုံထဲမှာ ရတနာသိုက်ရှိတယ် မိကျောင်းမျက်ရည်ဆိုတာ

အသားမစားသူတွေအတွက် အလကား ဟမ်ဘာဂါ ဆိုတဲ့ စာလုံးကို

အနက်ဖွင့်တာ လူမျိုးစုတစ်စုနဲ့တစ်စု မတူလို့ အဒီအရပ်မှာ

ပြည်တွင်းစစ် ဖြစ်တယ် ငါ့ ဟမ်ဘာဂါရဲ့ အောက်ဖက် အခြမ်းမှာလည်း

သွေးခြင်းခြင်းနီပဲ ကိုးမို့ရှင်ကို ကြောက်လို့ ကိုးယောက်စီး နွားလှည်း

တွေကို ကန့်သတ် ထားတယ် ဆပ်ပြာကောင်းကောင်း မတတ်နိုင်ရင်

ခေါင်းပေါင်းဖြူဖြူနဲ့ မထိုက်တန်ဘူး အမဲသားစားသူများ အသင်းဟာ

နွားအုပ်ကို နွားခြံထဲ မောင်းသွင်း နွားစာမြက်ကို ရှင်းပြီး တလင်းပြင်

ဖြစ်သွားတဲ့ နွားစားကျက်မှာ နွားစာပြောင်းမျိုးစေ့တွေကို ကျဲချလိုက်တယ်

And I should care? Why?

As sure as a cockcrow, brick and mortar will collapse. Treasure is found in a wasp nest. When the elders speak, youth listen.

During a tug-of-war to induce a downpour, it rained droves and droves of calves, still wet from the amniotic sac.

No petrichor when angles fall. Crocodile tears are not for vegans.

No two clans have the same definition for "hamburger." That's the reason for civil war. The flip side of my burger reads bloody rare.

In fear of the Lord of the Nine District Towns, ox carts with the seating capacity of nine passengers are banned.

On the prairie range cattle vacated, they have planted corn
for cattle.

The bottom line, they insist, is this:

If you can't afford decent detergent, you don't deserve a decent turban.

Final report by the Supreme People's Emergency Inquiry Commission [Classified]

1. Introduction

The Supreme People's Emergency Inquiry Commission (SPEIC), a team of twenty-four experts and concerned notables, was formed three years ago following the emergency motion to form the SPEIC was tabled and approved in Session 3 of The Supreme People's Assembly (SPA).

2. Objective

To investigate the causes of ongoing unrest in The Democratic Supreme People's Republic of Dukkha.

3. Principles

3a. Long-running development of The Democratic Supreme People's Republic of Dukkha
3b. Long-running benefit of her Supreme Citizens, i.e., the 135 national races and other breeds according to the Supreme People's Constitution and the Supreme State's existing Laws
3c. An optimally optimistic outlook for the long run

4. Methodology

Random sampling.
Note: In the field, "random sampling" turned out to be impractical as our researchers were unable to distinguish between the Randomers and Redeemers. Random sampling was dropped and replaced with "accidental sampling."

Sample question. Please tick the relevant box.

Are you with us?

☐ YES   ☐ YES, SIR!

5. Findings

5a. Almost all civil unrest has origins in communal brawls.
5b. All the victims who have succumbed to death suffered from fatal blows.
5c. The rage of the dispossessed has its roots in their dispossessedness.
5d. The laboratory test results of the water samples provided by the villagers from Copper Hill region confirms that the water from the *avici* wells in the area looks like urine, smells like urine and tastes like urine.
5e. Hillbillies do not want their hills to be destroyed.
5f. Population is a tragedy of the common, and a comedy of the uncommon.

5g. During the supreme rule of The Supreme Peace and Development Council that preceded the democratically elected government of the Democratic Supreme People's Republic of Dukkha, sulphuric acid was used widely.

6. Conclusions and Recommendations

6a. The lack of transparency is the root cause of the problem.
6b. It is highly recommended that transparency be upgraded immediately.

The Supreme People's Emergency Inquiry Commission
The Democratic Supreme People's Republic of Dukkha

Flex it gently and stretch it again

[Excerpts from the Speech by the President of The Democratic Supreme People's Republic of Dukkha to The Council for the Restoration of Freedom of the Press on the Occasion of World Literature Day]

Comrades . . . Our nation has existed since time immemorial when the lands were common to all mankind. So has our organization. Our people as well as the whole world can attest to countless selfless sacrifices made by members of our organization. Yet this very special occasion calls on me to reiterate all the self-denial we have made for this country for the sake of our people.

Comrades . . . We have kissed the lips of prison and struggled rain or shine for the sake of our national races and for the emancipation of the people from British colonial rule via the Fascist Japanese occupation towards the very Myanmar state properly ruled by parliamentary bigwigs and their cronies.

Comrades . . . Our sacrifice does not mean that we covet power, influence or wealth. Nor do we want people to worship us. No! Not at all! Nor do we want to gloat over our altruistic sacrifices for our nation and her nationals until our mouth soars as every opportunity arises. People know of our exemplary conduct, our solidarity, our unity and our transparency.

In this transitional era, we, who have given ourselves up to the nation through and through for many many many years, are afforded no leisure.

To serve the people to the utmost of our ability, we must catch up with the times, and continue to shoulder our historic responsibility diligently and unwaveringly. Inasmuch as our guidance and interventions are required by the people in all corners of the country, we, leaders, also must endure extreme hardship and humility in foreign lands when we go abroad to plead for development aid on behalf of our people.

By offering our lives, sweat and blood, we have rescued the motherland who was drowning in the shallows at the hands of human traffickers. We have annihilated stooges of the West. We have also lynched scores of terrorist-rapists and stoned to death some women of questionable reputation.

Through our struggles that entail countless self-denials, we have come to realize that there has not been any organization as fit and battle-hardened as ours in promoting the best interest of our nation. History calls on us that we carry on with our sacrifice, by risking our lives if need be, and continue our pro bono efforts for the whole nation by turning ourselves into a political party no matter how much we despise politics.

Comrades . . . You are all aware of our conviction, commitment and principles. I need not elaborate further all the details of the sacrifices made by us leaders—our nation and the whole world can attest to our courage.

Comrades . . . Time is a luxury we cannot afford.

I would like to end here by earnestly urging you to live up to
our organization's historic legacy, do as you are told along the
chain of command and, above all, for the sake of chest-to-
chest national harmony, seek and destroy your nearest enemy
with any available weapons. If you are not already armed,
remove the elastic band from your underwear and turn it into a
slingshot!

Onward we march! Victory is ours!

ကက်ကြေး-စက္ကူ-ကျောက်တုံး

ရေးတော့အမှန် ဖတ်တော့အသံ ဆိုတဲ့ အရေးစကားဟာ
အပြောစကားရဲ့ အသိံထွက်ကို မှန်အောင် စာလုံးမပေါင်းနိုင်ရှာဘူး
အပြောစကားကလည်း အလုပ်လောက် တာမသွားဘူး
အဲဒါကြောင့် လူကြုပ်တဲ့ လောကကြီးထဲ
တံတောင်နဲ့တွတ်တဲ့ ခရီးသည်တွေ ပြည့်နေတာ
လူတွေ ဖန်တီးထားတဲ့ ဘာသာစကားဟာ
လူတွေ ဖန်တီးထားတဲ့ နာကျင်မှုကို ဖော်ပြဖို့ မလုံလောက်
အပစ်အခတ်ရပ်စဲရေး စာချုပ်တွေ ဘယ်လောက်လက်မှတ်ထိုးထိုး
သေနတ်ပြောင်းဝတွေဟာ အကျယ်ဆုံးပါးစပ်ပေါက်တွေအနေနဲ့ ကျန်နေဦးမှာ
တိုနေ့က ငါ့ကို အုပ်စုလိုက် မုဒိမ်းကျင့်သွားတဲ့ မင့်မျက်လုံးတွေ
အဲဒီ နာကျင်မှုဟာ တကယ်လား စိတ်ကူးယဉ်လား
ငါ ပြန်မပြောပြတတ် ငါ ပြန်ပြောပြတတ်ရင်တောင် ငါ ချမရေးတတ်
ခု ငါ ချရေးနေတာတွေကိုက ငါ ပြောချင်တာတွေနဲ့ တခြားစီ
ငါ ပြောနိုင်တာတွေကလည်း ငါ့နာကျင်မှုကို ကိုယ်စားမပြု
အမှုအရာ စကား စာတွေနဲ့ လူအချင်းချင်း စတင် ဆက်သွယ်ကြ
ကတည်းက လူတွေဟာ ကက်ကြေး-စက္ကူ-ကျောက်တုံး ကစားလာခဲ့
ကျောက်တုံးက ကက်ကြေးကို အမဲ့ နိုင်တယ်
ကက်ကြေးက စက္ကူကို အမဲ့ နိုင်တယ်
စက္ကူက ကျောက်တုံးကို နိုင်တယ်ဆိုရင်လည်း
အဲဒီ စက္ကူဟာ ကျောက်တုံးရဲ့ မကျော့မှုကို ဖုံးဖိ
ကွယ်ဝှက်ပေးထားတဲ့ ထုပ်ပိုးစက္ကူပဲ
ဒီကစားနည်းရဲ့ စည်းမျဉ်း ဘယ်အခါမှ မပြောင်းလဲ

Scissors-paper-stone

The world is packed with passengers who elbow each other all the time. The verbal "Excuse me" or texted "Excuse me" will not suffice.

Human language is simply inadequate for human pain.

The number of ceasefire accords notwithstanding, gun barrels will remain mouthier than mouths, saltier than salt.

To hear the ocean roar you've got to see the ocean.

What I say will always be a remote description of my Weltschmerz.

For yonks, stone has beaten scissors. Scissors have beaten paper.

Paper beats stone only as a wrapper, the furtive concealer of callousness.

The rules of the game don't change.

They never will.

ခရီးသွားမှတ်တမ်း

ဘာမှမထူး လူတကာ ရောက်ဖူးတဲ့နေရာတွေ
ခြေကျင်တလှည့် မြင်းနဲ့တဖုံ
တောအထပ်ထပ် တောင်အသွယ်သွယ်
ဒီလိုပဲ သွားခဲ့ ဒီလိုပဲ နေခဲ့
စိတ်လှုပ်ရှားလွယ်သူတွေအတွက်တော့ စိတ်လှုပ်ရှားစရာ အပြည့်
ငါ့ အတွက်တော့ တယ် ထူးလှတယ်မရှိ
အားလုံး အဆင်ပြေချောမွေ့ပါတယ်
အဆင်မပြေတာတွေလည်း ရှိပါ
တကယ့်အကြီးကြီးလို့ထင်ခဲ့တဲ့ ရေတံခွန်ဟာ အပြင်မှာ ထင်သလောက်မကြီး
စပါးအုံးမွေးသူက တစ်လံလောက်ရှိတဲ့ သူအချစ်တော်ကို
လည်ပင်းစွဲပြီး လူတွေကြားထဲ လျှောက်သွားနေတာ
လူပုံပူဖောင်းရုပ်ကလေးတွေ ရောင်းတဲ့ ဆရာမရဲ့
လက်ထဲ လူရုပ်လေးတွေ အများကြီး
ငါးမျှားတံလိုတုတ်နဲ့ သူကိုင်ထားတာက တစ်ရုပ်တည်း
တုတ်ကို ဆွဲမလိုက်တိုင်း
အရုပ်က အသက်ဝင်လာပြီး လက်ဟန်ခြေဟန်တွေ လုပ်ပြ
အရုပ်ကလေးကို အပဲ့နဲ့သွားကလိတာ
ဖောင်းကနဲ့ပေါက်သွားလို့ ရော်ခဲ့ရ
မြို့လယ်ခေါင် ရင်ပြင်မှာ ကော်ဇောခင်းပြီး
လေပေါ်မှာ တင်ပလ္လင်ခွေထိုင်ပြတဲ့ ဆရာ
မျက်လှည့်ဆိုတာ သိသိကြီးနဲ့ လူတွေ ပါးစပ်အဟောင်းသား
သူ့ရှေ့က ခွက်ထဲ ပိုက်ဆံတွေ အပြည့်

Journey for a journal

The Humongous Falls aren't really that humongous. The
Border Guards are that nasty. The view from the other side is
perfect. Here's a haywire wire-haired *sadu* pushing through
the crowded market naked, a fathom-length python hanging
around his neck. A gypsy woman hawks little balloon-men.
When the woman waves her wand the balloon-men wank
in unison. I poke a balloon-man with my compass needle.
The balloon bursts. Semen splutters everywhere. Even after
I pay for the damage the woman looks weepy-sullen. On the
city square a man levitates, sitting cross-legged in the thin
air above a Persian rug. The bowl in front of him brims with
blurbs. In pilgrims' hands are invocations for sins, and alms
for auspices. Angles aren't just deaf mutes. They are invisible.
Pigeons usually have tenure near city halls. The only way to
deal with their cackle is to sneeze extremely loud in their
midst. Angels' pinkish-pallid-translucent skin reminds me of
pigeon feet. Led by a guide I am being marched along in neck
shackles. When you need a loo, Turkish loos are everywhere.
Djinns take human form as tourists. The way poets speak
about their own poems parents talk about their children.
Excuse me! The aisle seat is mine. The armrest is mine. The
authentic baggage is mine. I am not into bondage. I prefer
light travel. I've followed someone into a late Middle Age
Gothic church. I found the lineaments of saints lamentably

ဘုရားဖူးတွေလက်ထဲ တွေ့နေကျ
အပြစ်လွှတ် ဆုတောင်းတွေ ကြီးပွားရေး အလှူငွေတွေ
ကဗျာဆရာတွေ သူတို့ကိုယ်တိုင်ရေးကဗျာတွေအကြောင်း ပြောသလို
မိဘတွေ အမြဲပြောတတ်တာက
သူတို့ ရင်သွေးလေးတွေ ချစ်စရာ ကောင်းကြောင်း လိမ္မာကြောင်း ထက်မြက်ကြောင်း
ဘုစုခရုတွေ မလိုချင်တဲ့ အပြင်
သူတို့ဝန်ကင်းလို့ တော်သေးရဲ့ တွေးမိ
ပေါ့ပေါ့ပါးပါး ခရီးသွားရတာကို ပိုသဘောကျတယ်
အကြမ်းဖက်ဖို့ သက်သက်လာတဲ့ လေးင်းယောက်ကတော့
ကြမ်းပေမပေါ့ ရမ်းပေမပေါ့
ဘာဆန်းလဲ
စစ်ပွဲ တစ်ပွဲ နှစ်ပွဲ ဖြတ်ရတုန်း ကိုယ့်ဒုက္ခမှ ကိုယ့်ဒုက္ခလို့ ထင်ခဲ့
သောက်ခဲ့ စားခဲ့ ငတ်ခဲ့ ပြတ်ခဲ့တာလည်း အများလိုပါပဲ
အလယ်ခေတ်နှောင်းပိုင်း ဂိုထစ်ဘုရားကျောင်းကြီးတွေ
သူများတွေ ဝင်ကြည့်လို့ ဝင်ကြည့်ခဲ့
ဟိုတယ်ခန်းတွေ ဇိမ်ခံကားတွေ အများပိုင်ယာဉ်တွေ
ဘယ်နေရာမှာမဆို တူတူပဲ
ပြတိုက်တွေထဲ မကုန်နိုင်မခမ်းနိုင် ရီနေဆန်းပန်းချီကားတွေ
တွေ့ရပါများလွန်းလို့ ခေါင်းနောက်လာ
မြေအောက်မြစ် ဖြတ်ဆင်းနေတဲ့ လှိုက်ဂူမှောင်မှောင်ကြီးတစ်ခုထဲက ဆင်ဖနီတီးဝိုင်း
ဘုရင်နဲ့ ဆွေတော်မျိုးတော်တွေ ရက်ရက်စက်စက်
အသတ်ခံလိုက်ရတဲ့ နန်းတော်
ရန်ဖြစ်ခဲ့တာ တစ်ခါ နှစ်ခါ
နေရာတွေ နာမည်တွေ မမှတ်မိတော့

symmetrical. A handful of terrorists in the guise of tourists lies in wait. What's new? The terrorists are there to terrorize the tourists who are there to terrorize the locals. Once I gave a treadmill a try. Years after I got off from it my legs are still in run mode, my Achilles tendons irreparably wrecked. The sheen of my spleen is green. My blood is tainted. Not life-threatening. Not yet. My doppelganger is a motherfucker. When I see the motherfucker I will draw lightning-fast, I'll shoot him dead. Some places can square watermelons. Some places sell bananas only by the bunch. Some people go in for cremation. Some people are cool with live burial. In Elysian Fields a mouse will take lightly a teasing elephant. From a blimp up high I once saw people plug into a national grid. Falling out of love is hard, falling for betrayal is worse. Impossible! Once I get back on solid ground I realize not every view from a great height is necessarily correct. Every place is fun to begin with. No souvenir is for keeps in the end. I am sorry to disappoint, but my journey isn't that of the five-year-old street urchin who found a new home in a galaxy far far away, and twenty light years later, time-travelled back to the earth, to be reunited with his mother in his village of birth. Not that I don't miss you, mom. Mine isn't really much. It's just an average experience.

အလကားရလို့ အပြေးစက်ပေါ် အတော်ကြာ တက်ပြေးကြည့်တော့
စက်ပေါ်က ဆင်းလိုက်တာတောင် ခြေထောက်တွေက အပြေးအလွှားစိတ်မကုန်
တချို့အရပ်တွေမှာ ဖရဲသီးတောင် ေလးထောင့်ပုံ ဖြစ်အောင် ပုံစံသွင်းကြ
မီးပုံးပုံကြီး တက်စီးတုန်းခဏ
အရာရာကို အပေါ် စီးက ရှင်းရှင်းလင်းလင်း မြင်ခဲ့
အပေါ် စီးက မြင်တဲ့ အမြင်တိုင်းဟာ
မမှန်ဘူးဆိုတာ အောက်ပြန်ရောက်မှ သိခဲ့
ဘယ်လောက် ပျင်းစရာကောင်းတဲ့ နေရာမဆို
ရောက်ခါစမှာ ပျော်စရာ
အသည်းကွဲခဲ့တာ တစ်ခါနှစ်ခါ
ချစ်ကွဲညား တစ်ခါဒါဇင်မက
အမွေကိုတော့ သတိရပါ့
အမွေသားဇာတ်လမ်းက မိဘမွဲပျိုကျကလေးတစ်ယောက်
အလင်းနှစ်များစွာ ကွာဝေးတဲ့ ဂြိုဟ်တခုပေါ် ရောက်သွား
ကောင်းစားပြီး ဖမချိန်ခက်ကြီးကိုစီး မွေးရပ်မြေပြန်တဲ့ ဇာတ်မဟုတ်တော့
ဘာဆို ဘာမှမထူး
လူတကာ အတွေ့အကြုံထက် တပြားသားမှ မပိ

Bloody tongue [at language's edge]

[1]

The edge of language is the edge of the adhesive seal of an envelope you lick to en-coffin the corpse of a poem you wish you had never written. While tonguing and wetting the triangular edge of the envelope, you don't realize your tongue is cut. By the time you sense a taste of warm salty-musty liquid on your palate, it's too late. Squeamish as you are, you have already swallowed the blood of your own tongue. I am talking about a bloody tongue.

[2]

When the mother tongue embraces you like a failed state, she will never let you off. Bloody tongue, they say, is the sword of destiny against "the wooden tongue" of tyranny. Yet, history has proven that it is the bloody tongue that gets cut after cut after cut after cut after cut. Again and again and again and again.

[3]

Why are you having recurrent nightmares in which you are
thrown into a ring to find yourself wrestling with the two post-
modern Goliaths: the mode of production of poetry and the
commodification of poetry?

[4]

you've come out of the closet
the closet is crowded

Yet you can't escape. Everywhere you want to go—margin,
conceptual, post-conceptual, alternative, queer, underground is
packed. Your presence in the margin is not welcome. You have
just become another widening factor for the very margin which
has now invaded the main page.

You do what a wolf does when it finds a goat hide. It chews on
it while sleeping on it.

[5]

how do you write history
in a language that has no
past tense?

[6]

You say bloody tongue is a silver bullet for what you call "creative angst."
Once you suggested to a poet with writer's block that he betray his own
bloody tongue. Just go out on a date with another bloody tongue, you
said. How did a poet end up with writer's block in the first place?

[7]

What do you do when your first bloody tongue says, "I have a book," and
the second one says, "There is a book inside me." Your mother tongue
says, "I go to school." Your second tongue insists, it should be "I school
to go." Each time you utter a sentence, your second bloody tongue utters
another sentence in inversion. The split of your bloody tongue will turn
your tongue into a snake tongue.

No worries. People will read you as if you were the Venomous, the
original.

[8]

Look what I've done to Maung Chaw Nwe's "Fish":

Fish

All my life
I've never caught a single perch
Look now,
the entire universe hangs twitching at the end of my line!
As I reel in the damn whale,
my rod
bends into a rainbow.
I turn into a fish

[9]

As far as I am concerned the most unpronounceable and
untranslatable word, yet the most useful cure for creative angst
is *Perkele*! *Perkele* means "devil" in Finnish. Some people believe
Perkele is the original name of Ukko, the Zeus of the Finnish pagan
pantheon. In what other language do we have a word that can mean
God and Devil at the same time? When you say "Perkele" in agony,
with a rolling *rrrrrrrrrr*, Satan and God will be at each other's
throat in their scramble to your rescue.

[10]

I may be able to Burmese my English. I may be able to English my Burmese. But I will not Finnish my Burmese. Nor my Burmese Finnish. *Perrrkele*!

[11]

1, 2, 3, 4, 5, 6, 7, 8, 9 . . .
၁၊ ၂၊ ၃၊ ၄၊ ၅၊ ၆၊ ၇၊ ၈၊ ၉ . . .

Numerals . . . , the most translatable.

[12]

The Samsara is long, and endless. And we don't have all day.

[13]

You ask your lover,

"What have we done to deserve this?"

"Poetry," she says.

Green chilli

In Southeast Asia the hottest chilli is the smallest.

She Who Dares Eyeball the Devas is the name. From the House of
Madame Jeanette, they don't wait until she turns red.

When you call her hot, your tongue is already on fire. And yet, your
mouth waters. Your breathing quickens, your face thickens, your senses
make no sense, death flashes in your temporal lobe, you will implode
and explode in turn, until your heart tugs at your head. And now, with
teary eyes, you regret the second you set eyes on her, "What have I done?"

What you have done cannot be undone.

Nothing personal. It's *not* taste, flavour or smell.

It's *mouthfeel*.

Green chilli burns twice. First, in Heaven. Much later—

in Hell.

Impermanence of paper

When a sheet of paper turns cranky, creamy, cracked and crisp, he
is a step away from the collapse in the bathroom, and hip replacement.

Some yellowed pages will never get up once they fall.

Some octogenarians get confined to bed in hospices for years
before they are reincarnated as toilet paper.

Don't take senescene for innocence. Death is disgusting.

Measures have been taken to immortalize paper. Acid-free paper
is permanent.

And yet even the permanent grade breaks down in days—

under the tyranny of termites.

People in the picture

She who is in the centre of a group photo always smiles miles higher than those around her.

Only when you are in the centre of a group picture you smile like she who is in the centre of a group picture.

That explains the gravitational pull of the centre. The more people from the margin push towards the centre the more the centre loses centrality.

No lens of history is inclusive enough to keep everyone in the picture. An extremely long shot is necessary if everyone wants to be in the picture.

In an extremely long shot people resemble matchsticks. Matchsticks think everywhere is the centre.

In any group photo, people's shadows can be seen inclining towards the centre. Knowingly or unknowingly people tend to move towards what they believe is the centre.

In so doing—

they move history with them.

ဒီမတိုင်ခင်

'ဒီနောက် [After That]' ရေးတဲ့
ရှုန်တာရိုတာနီကာဝါ [Shuntarō Tanikawa] အတွက်

ဒီမတိုင်ခင် အများကြီး ရှိသေးတယ်
ဒီစာမျက်နှာကို ရောက်ကို ရောက်ရမယ်ဆိုတဲ့ ယုံကြည်မှုတွေ
ဒါလုပ်ရင် ဒါဖြစ်ရမယ်ဆိုတဲ့ ကိန်းသေတွက်ကိန်းတွေ

ဘဝမှာ အရာရာ အဖြူ၊အမည်းသဲကွဲခဲ့
အမှားကို ဘယ်လက်နဲ့ အမှန်ကို ညာလက်နဲ့
ဒီလို ဆုပ်ကိုင်နိုင်ခဲ့

ဒီမတိုင်ခင်က ဒါကို ရရင်
တသက်လုံးပျော်ရွှင်နိုင်မယ် ဒီလို တွေးခဲ့
သေခြင်းကို သရေကွင်းလို ဆွဲဆန့်နိုင်မယ် ထင်ခဲ့
ဒီမတိုင်ခင်က ဒါကို ဒီလောက်ကောင်းမှန်း မသိခဲ့
အားလုံးက သူ့ကို အသည်းမာသူလို့ ထင်ခဲ့

မြူခိုးတွေကတော့ ဒီမတိုင်ခင်ရော ဒီနောက်ရော
ပိန်းပိတ်အောင်ကျနေဆဲ

ကမ်းခြေမှာ ဇင်ယော်တွေ တအာအာနဲ့ —

ယက်မအူသံ သူတစ်ယောက်တည်း ကြားခဲ့ရတယ်

Before that

after "After That" by Shuntarō Tanikawa

There were stories before that.

Determination told him he must reach there. Calculations
                    were always with lots of constants.

In life black and white were self-evident.

He was able to hold right in the right hand, and wrong in the left.
                    Just like that.

Before that, he thought, if he achieved that, he would be happy
                    ever after.

Death was an elastic band.

Before that he didn't realize it would be that tasty. Everyone
                    thought he had a heart hard-bitten.

Seagull squawks drowned out the roar of the ocean.

Through the scrim of the thick mist, not even half-light was cast

before that, and after that.

Acknowledgments

A number of poems that appear in *Bamboophobia* were written in Burmese. I have translated those poems into English for this collection.

I am profoundly grateful to the editors and staff members of the *Asia Literary Review, Bengal Lights, Be Untexed, Cha: An Asian Literary Journal, Cyphers, Granta, Griffith Review, International Writing Program Anthology: 2016* [The University of Iowa], *The Margins, Postscript, The Tiger Moth Review, Usawa Literary Review*, and *World Literature Today* for acknowledging my work. Very special thanks to Mara Genschel and Jonathan Stout for "Bloody tongue [at language's edge]," to John Wilcox for "Gust," Charles Bernstein for being *self-untaught*, Kelly Falconer for all the whiskey in heaven, Christopher Merrill for Iowa and Christopher Mattison for making things happen in Hong Kong.

I owe so much to family and friends; the Chuas of Choa Chu Kang, Daw Daw Chaw, Aunty Seng Raw, Aunty Wendy, Penny Edwards, Maw Shein Win, David Cole, Patricia Kelly, Soe Moe Latt, Bobo Lan Sin, Bobo Naung, Minh Bui Jones, Joseph Wood and Graeme Falconer for inspiration, love and support through the lockups and lockdowns of 2020 and 2021.

—*Ko Ko Thett, 2021*